FOUND THE GOD IN ME:

AN INNER WORK GUIDE TO RECLAIMING YOUR LIGHT

Madison Moss

Contents

For my younger self — enjoy every step of the journey.
One day you will look back and see how far you've come.

For my sister — thank you for walking with me through every
version of myself and loving me through them all.

And for my future children—

May you always find God within you.

To anyone who feels like they are stuck between who they once were
and who they are becoming — this is for you.

This is a journey of self-discovery and reclaiming your power.

The work you do internally, and the peace you cultivate from within
can never be taken away from you.

I am not writing from the finish line.
I'm writing from the middle of my journey.
I'm still growing. I'm still healing. I'm still learning.

These words do not belong to me — the wisdom is God's.
I'm simply the vessel He chose to carry it to you.

But they are mine in experience, because God is within me.

Finally free. Found the God in Me.

And you.

Part I: The Awakening

"The secret is not to chase butterflies...
It's to take care of the garden so that they come to you."
— Mário Quintan

And even if the butterflies don't come,
At least you still have a beautiful garden.

CHAPTER 1

TO THE ONE WHO WANTS MORE...

Before you begin reading, take a breath and ask yourself something honest...

Do you like where you currently are in life?

It's okay to want more for yourself. It's okay to be grateful for what you have, but to still long for something greater.

Any desire that's been placed in your heart is available for you. You are being called to rise to it.

God knows your deepest desires.
It's up to you to take aligned action.
It's up to you to stop delaying your blessings.

The longer you wait to build the future you want, the less time you will have to spend in it.

Ask yourself:

Do my habits align with the life I want?
Do my friends reflect the person I want to become?
Am I being intentional with my time?
Am I leaking energy in places that no longer serve me?
Am I saying "yes" when I really mean "no"?
Am I more focused on pleasing others than stepping into my purpose?

Whatever you desire was placed in your heart by the God of infinite possibilities.
If you weren't meant to have it, you wouldn't have felt called to it.
Some might call it delusional — but I call it **faith**.

> *"You don't have enough faith," Jesus told the*
> *m. "I tell you the truth, if you had faith even*
> *as small as a mustard seed, you could say to*
> *this mountain, 'Move from here to there,' and it*
> *would move. Nothing would be impossible."*
> — Matthew 17:20

Are you giving God the opportunity to reveal what He has for you?
Or are you too distracted by the noise of the world to hear His voice?

The crowd is lost — we must follow God.

When was the last time you let your mind be still long enough to listen?

When was the last time you prayed,
"God, show me what You have for me.
I'm willing to do whatever it takes."

Sometimes clarity comes in whispers.
But you must quiet your mind to hear it.

You may never have all of the answers.
But He will always reveal the next step.

The goal isn't to predict the path —
it's to trust the One who made it.

To the one who wants more...

You must start by finding your purpose, and cut out whatever doesn't align with it. Align with the frequency of who you want to be.

Surround yourself with people who honor your presence.
Be intentional about who gets access to you.

Be honest with yourself: In what areas of your life are you choosing short-term pleasure over long-term peace?

"Let us not become weary in doing good, for at the proper time we will reap a harvest if we do not give up." — Galatians 6:9

You can choose to up level, or you can stay stuck — in the same places, with the same people, repeating the same patterns.

Is it possible that the reason you haven't changed is because you know it would mean raising your standards, cutting off certain people, and becoming more disciplined?

Are you ready to break habits and cycles that have kept you stuck?

Do you truly know your worth?

Do you recognize your full potential?

Are you living in alignment with the old you — or where you want to go?

Like tuning into a radio station, you can tune in to different versions of your reality.
You do this through your frequency.

You can't see radio waves with your eyes — but they are real.
Just like the frequency you're sending out into the world.

Your frequency determines the daily events of your life.

Tune in to the frequency of who you want to be, not who you once were.

How would that version of you spend their free time?
What would they be watching?
What would they be eating?
How would they feel when they got out of bed in the morning?
Would they be grateful for what they currently have?

Do the things that version of you would be doing — and *feel* the things they'd be feeling.

You cannot outrun your frequency.

What you consider reality (3D, life on Earth) will never change unless you first change your frequency.

You cannot bring something into your physical reality that you haven't already decided in your mind.

> *"Your kingdom come, your will be done,*
> *on earth as it is in heaven."*
> — Matthew 6:10

"On earth as it is in heaven"...
Let my thoughts, feelings, and imagination create a *heaven state* through prayer and meditation.

Let this heaven state of mind be reflected on earth in your daily life.

When your mindset is aligned with faith, love, and purpose, your life on earth will start to reflect that.

Trust God's plan, and have faith that everything will work out.

But remember: **faith requires discipline**.

You still have to make choices that bring you closer to the person you've been called to be.

All paths lead you to where you're meant to be.
Your choices determine how long it takes to get there.

You have free will — and you can delay your own blessings.
Sometimes, the things that delay us aren't always obvious.
Some moments that seem harmless — distractions, temptations, compromises — can pull us out of alignment with God's plan.

Nothing will derail what God wants to do in and through you faster than sin. So eliminate the moments in your life that lead up to the moments of sin.

Sin feels good in the moment, but resisting sin keeps you in alignment with God's plan.

He is working in your life — don't get in the way.

"Throw off your old sinful nature and your former way of life, which is corrupted by lust and deception. Instead, let the Spirit renew your thoughts and attitudes."
— Ephesians 4:22–24

To the one who wants more...

You are ambitious.
You have big goals.
I admire you for that.
But what actions are you taking?

What has God placed on your heart that you've been avoiding?

Sometimes, what you are avoiding is exactly what is necessary to bring you to the next level.

If you knew for a fact you were going to receive everything you desire two weeks from now...
What would you start doing today to prepare for it?

Would you waste your time scrolling on social media, being unproductive?

Or would you get up and do what needs to be done to become the version of you who's ready for those blessings?

If you received everything you want right now —
Would you truly be ready for it?

There is no perfect time to change.

The time is now.

The version of you you've been praying for can be built by the choices you make today.

You've waited long enough...

Decide now that you are ready for more.

Say it out loud:

"I am ready for more."

Chapter 2

My Awakening

There are years of my life I have little to no memory of.

It requires emotion for your brain to process and store memories.
Highly emotionally charged experiences tell your brain that the information is necessary for survival, so it stores it as a long-term memory.

There was a point in my life that I was living entirely in my head.
I felt numb.
I was not *present* enough to experience emotions deeply, which meant I created few long-term memories.

I was convinced something was wrong with me.
I was emotionally disconnected. Frozen.

I remember going over a year without crying.
Not because I was happy, but because I felt nothing at all.

I went through several self diagnosis processes, googling my symptoms daily, and constantly telling my friends, *"I don't feel real"*.

I even hired a therapist, and 5 minutes into our conversation, she said, "I'm sorry Madison, but I have no idea how to help you with the symptoms you've described."

My childhood friend had passed away. I knew I was sad. I knew I should have been crying. But I was so numb, so detached, that I could not even shed a tear.

That day I realized that something was not right.
It was like I was there... but I wasn't.

I remember feeling so alone, even when I was surrounded by people.
Feeling like no one would ever understand me.
No one ever noticed. Everyone thought I was perfectly fine.

Later, I would learn that everything I was feeling had a name.
One day, while searching for answers, I stumbled across a video about depersonalization and derealization.

In short, depersonalization is when you feel disconnected from yourself, like you are watching yourself from the outside, and derealization is when you feel disconnected from the world around you.

At that time I thought— *well I guess I have both. But at least now I know other people have experienced this too!*

None of my friends, family, or even therapists had understood what I was feeling, but now that I knew I wasn't alone, I already felt better.

I made a decision that day, that I don't have to feel this way anymore.

I wanted to find out the root cause, and I was relieved, and somewhat annoyed to find out that the reason for years of my life feeling wasted was nothing more than:

Anxiety.

You have probably heard the phrase "fight or flight".

The fight or flight response is simply the way our bodies react when our nervous system perceives a threat or danger— real or imagined.

When your body feels threatened, it goes into one of two modes:

1. **Fight:** Confront the threat— physically, or mentally by arguing and becoming defensive.

2. **Flight:** Escape the threat—by running away, avoiding, or emotionally shutting down.

There are 2 more modes that are less talked about— freeze and fawn.

1. **Freeze:** Your mind gets stuck. You feel overwhelmed, paralyzed, or emotionally numb.

2. **Fawn:** You try to please the threat to stay safe—agreeing to things you don't want to do or people-pleasing.

I was living in a state of functional freeze that was rooted in anxiety.

Anxiety is your brain perceiving a threat when you are not actually in danger.

Being in a constant state of fight, flight, freeze or fawn is called living in **survival mode**.

It is necessary to enter these states sometimes to keep you safe, or *survive*, but it is no way to live your life.

So, how do we reduce anxiety?

There are many ways, the first being the most important: faith in God.

> *"Do not be anxious about anything, but in every situation, by prayer and petition, with thanksgiving, present your requests to God. And the peace of God, which transcends all understanding, will guard your hearts and your minds in Christ Jesus."* — Philippians 4:6–7

Anxiety holds no power over you when you know God is within you.
Look back on your life...
Has God not gotten you through every situation you have ever faced?

It's not blind faith—it is conviction with evidence to back it up.
Every storm you ever thought would break you, he carried you through.

"One set of footsteps in the sand, He was carrying me." — Kanye West

Is it not insulting to God when you stress about something he has already made a way for?

Faith does not mean you will never feel afraid.
It means you choose to trust in the plan even when you are afraid.

> *"When I am afraid, I put my trust in You."*
> — Psalm 56:3

The next step is to heal your nervous system.
Your nervous system is your body's alarm system. It's designed to protect you.
But as we already explored, sometimes it gets stuck "on" even when there is nothing threatening you.

Healing your nervous system is about reminding your body that you are safe.
You can teach your body that it is safe to live in peace instead of survival mode.

There are many ways you can do this—prayer, meditation, mindfulness, breathwork, affirmations, listening to healing frequencies—some of which will be explored in more detail in a later chapter.

When peace becomes your default state, your nervous system is no longer in overdrive.

You gain clarity on what triggers your stress—and the power to remove those situations and people from your life.

From this grounded place, you reclaim your energy and reconnect with your intuition.

You feel safe in your body.

You become fully present.

At peace within, you make better decisions, hear your inner voice clearly, and feel God speaking to you.

But remember: it is impossible to make these changes in your life without first becoming self aware of your inner state.

Are you stuck in survival mode?

Let this be your awakening.

Chapter 3

Inner Work

Inner work is the process of turning inward so you can live more aligned with your highest self.

It is becoming self aware and taking the initiative to change.

It's recognizing the thoughts that don't serve you, the beliefs that were never really yours, and the patterns that keep you stuck.

And then choosing to rewrite them.

Inner work is when you finally stop trying to be understood by the world, and start trying to understand yourself.

Your outer world is a direct reflection of your inner world.

Your inner world is the cause.

And your reality is the effect.

Doing inner work is like cleaning your house.

You don't just clean it once and it's clean forever.

Things get messy again, you clean again, and the cycle continues...

It's the ongoing practice of:

Becoming aware of thought patterns and behaviors you've outgrown
Identifying and correcting limiting beliefs
Healing emotional wounds and traumas
Responding rather than reacting
Releasing shame, guilt, and self-judgment
Practicing mindfulness, presence, and self-compassion
Strengthening your connection to God

I truly believe I get to have it all in every area of my life— love, peace, finances, purpose.
But trying to focus on everything at once left me overwhelmed and stuck.

Five years ago, I focused all my energy on my fitness journey. That one choice introduced me to life-changing friendships and connections that led me to my church, and even helped me manifest my dream apartment.

That's the power of focus.
When you give your full attention to one area, there is a ripple effect into every area of your life.

Inner work is the key to unlocking your next level in life.

It helps you to understand why you are the way that you are.
It helps you to align your frequency with who you want to become.

Ask yourself: "What area of my life, if I gave it my full attention, would make the biggest difference right now?"

Is it getting back in the gym?
Going to church?
Building a consistent morning routine?
Healing your trauma?

Tune in and decide what feels most important for *this* season of your life.
If you're unsure where to begin, we will cover some daily practices in the next chapter.

> **"If you don't know what to pursue in life right now, pursue yourself. Pursue becoming the healthiest, happiest, most healed, most present, most confident version of yourself. Then the right path will reveal itself."** —Unknown

Some people have deeper wounds to tend to — so your first step may be finding a therapist.

But for many, the process can begin today by simply noticing your triggers.

A **trigger** is like scratching an open wound — it brings something up that hasn't fully healed.
Start noticing what makes you feel defensive, irritated, or upset.

Anytime you are triggered by someone not intentionally trying to hurt you, there is an opportunity for healing in that area.
There's likely something deeper there that's calling for your attention.

Write it down. Get curious about it.

What's the root cause?

Where did that feeling come from?

What's one actionable step to take to start healing?

Here's a personal example:

I used to be cripplingly shy.

I admired outgoing people and wished I could be more like them.

So when someone said, "Why are you so quiet?" or "Why don't you ever dance?" — it hurt.

Not because they were being mean.

But because they were pointing out something I didn't like about myself.

So let's break it down:

Trigger: Being called quiet or boring.

Root: I don't want to be shy anymore.

Action: Work on confidence or accept myself as I am and embrace it.

It's not the world's job to tiptoe around your unhealed wounds.

It's your job to become aware of them and take the steps to heal.

Someone ready for transformation doesn't avoid their triggers, they welcome them.

Because they know **every trigger is an opportunity to grow**.

You don't have to heal everything at once.

Just start.

Inner work is the root.

Everything else grows from there.

When you heal your inner world, your entire life will begin to shift.

Journal Prompts:

What area of my life do I feel most called to focus on right now?

What makes me feel triggered?

What thought, belief, or behavior have I outgrown—but keep repeating out of habit or comfort?

CHAPTER 4

SACRED DAILY PRACTICES

It takes, on average, **66 days to form a habit**.
Don't overwhelm yourself—start small.

Choose **1-3 daily practices** that resonate with you most.
Stick with them, and build the foundation first.
Then layer in more.

And remember:
If you have more than three priorities, you have none.
Trying to change everything at once will keep you stuck.

The most important step is **self-awareness**.
What area of your life needs the most attention right now?

These are the practices that have made the biggest difference in mine.

$$\diamond \ \diamond \ \diamond$$

Be Intentional In the Morning

Most people wake up and immediately check their phone.

But why open Instagram before thanking God for waking you up?

Jay Shetty once asked:

Would you allow 100 people into your bedroom to start talking the moment you open your eyes?

Of course not—it would feel overwhelming and chaotic.

Yet that's exactly what we do when we start the day on social media.

We flood our minds with outside noise: opinions, comparisons, false information, and negative news.

That is no way to begin your day if your goal is a clear mind and peaceful nervous system.

When you first wake up, before you are fully alert, your brain is in a hypnopompic state. In this state your mind is more open to influence.

Be intentional about what you feed your mind during this time.

Go to God first.

Start your day with stillness and presence.
You deserve that.
Your nervous system will thank you.

Start your day with gratitude and prayer.
He deserves that.

Ask God to guide your day before the world has a chance to influence it.

"Very early in the morning, while it was still dark, Jesus got up, left the house and went off to a solitary place, where he prayed." — Mark 1:35

GRATITUDE

Showing gratitude is a sure way to raise your vibration.
It emits one of the highest frequencies you can embody.

When you're in a high vibe emotional state, you become a **magnet** for more good.

It shifts your brain to focus on what you have — not what's missing.

We have touched on this:

You can only manifest into 3D what you first already believe and **feel** internally.

If you are constantly stuck in the feeling of "lack", you will continue to attract more experiences that reflect that lack.

**When you show gratitude for what you already have,
You invite more to be grateful for.**

Look at your life.

Recognize that you're currently living in answered prayers.

If you have the means to buy this book, a safe place to sleep, clean water, and internet access, you are more fortunate than the majority of the world—and likely in the top 10% globally in terms of access to basic resources.

Let this awareness lead you into deeper gratitude.

Your *normal day* is someone else's *dream*, so be thankful.

Gratitude honors God.

It aligns you with abundance.

Recognize God as the source of your blessings, and you will surely receive more.

> *"Give thanks in all circumstances; for this is*
> *God's will for you in Christ Jesus."*
> — 1 Thessalonians 5:18

MEDITATION

Meditation is simply the practice of being still and tuning into your inner world.
It helps quiet your thoughts.
It brings your attention back to the present moment,
And it helps you reconnect with yourself and God.

When you *try* to meditate, it will feel hard. That's normal.
But there's no effort that should be put into it. **Just be.**

Watch your thoughts come and go like clouds drifting by.

You can focus on your inhales and exhales, or repeat a mantra, phrase, or verse to help guide your attention back when your mind wanders.

Let it be the intentional practice of removing your attention from the external — the illusions of the world that have so many people in a chokehold — and turning inward to awaken the God within you.

Anything done with presence can become meditation.

Washing dishes. Sitting in silence. Even walking.

I vividly remember my first meditation experience.
I was sitting in the sauna— the only 15 minutes a day I didn't have my phone. I focused on my breath and watched my thoughts.
And for the first time, my mind went still.
It became the part of my day I craved most.
I started to realize my best ideas, deepest truths, and biggest spiritual downloads came after I meditated.
And that I could access that stillness anywhere, anytime.

Meditation separates yourself from what your mind is telling you.
Not every thought you have is your own.
Become the witness of your subconscious programming, and the lies it tells you.

Let your higher self become the witness of what your lower self is trying to tell you.

Meditation allows you to starve out the lower self by not entertaining those thoughts anymore.
It allows you to tap in to your higher self where positivity, creativity, and abundance flows.

LIVING IN THE PRESENT

Being present is one of the most powerful tools for a joyful life.

Focusing on the past leads to sadness or regret.
Focusing on the future can cause anxiety and fear.
But **the present moment is where you can find peace.**

It's simply getting out of your head and being where your feet are.

You can't reach out and touch the past, and the future hasn't happened yet.   The past and future are just thoughts.
But the present?
It's here, now. It's real and tangible.

When you stop and think about your problems, are they happening *right now*, or are they based in some future "what if"?
Most of our stress is rooted in imagination— not reality.

Let go of control. Give it to God.

Start by noticing your surroundings. Use your senses.
What do you see?
What do you hear?
What do you feel?

Be fully alive in this moment.

Life happens in the present.

The first time I felt it, I was lying in a hammock, reading *The Power of Now* by Eckhart Tolle. The book told me to stop. Be fully present in this moment.

And in that stillness, I felt a warmth, a lightness, a deep inner peace.
It was a feeling beyond words.
A knowing that this was what I'd been missing.

Since then, I've practiced presence as much as possible, and it has slowly become my default state.
Not perfect.
But more happy and at peace than I've ever been.

> *"Therefore do not worry about tomorrow, for tomorrow will worry about itself. Each day has enough trouble of its own."* — Matthew 6:34

Affirmations

Affirmations are short, powerful statements you repeat to rewire your mind.

They replace the thoughts that hold you back with thoughts that lift you up.

Say them. Write them. Listen to them.
Let them become your new inner dialogue.

The more you repeat them — with feeling — the more your brain forms new neural pathways.

Over time, those thoughts become your new mindset, and start to shape your identity.

One of the most powerful times to listen to affirmations is at night while you sleep.

When you're in deep rest, your brain slows down into theta and delta waves — and that's when your subconscious is most open.
You're not overthinking. You're not resisting. You're just receiving.

Say "I am rich" at 3 PM and your ego might argue.
Say it in your sleep... and your brain just absorbs it.

Remember, consistency is key when using affirmations.

It is backed by psychological research that the more you tell yourself something, the more likely you are to believe it.

Repetition strengthens neural pathways.

What you subconsciously believe about yourself shapes your entire life.

It influences every decision you make, whether you realize it or not.

Affirmations help reprogram your self-concept and align you with your highest self.

"The tongue has the power of life and death, and those who love it will eat its fruit."
— Proverbs 18:21

VISUALIZATION

Visualization is a mental rehearsal of your future.
It's the movie you play in your mind — with **you** as the lead.

While repetition can program your subconscious overtime,
emotion has the power to do it faster.

Visualize you as your highest self— you at your happiest, most
peaceful, most successful.
The goal is to **see it**, **feel it**, and **believe it**.
Down to the details:
What are you wearing?
What do you smell like?
How do you feel in that moment?

The clearer the image, the more familiar it becomes.
And the more familiar it feels, the more likely your brain is to believe
it, and act on it.

Your subconscious doesn't fully distinguish between imagined and real experiences.

That's why **visualizing** consistently can align your body and mind with a new reality —before it arrives.

You are creating feelings— validation, love, appreciation, joy — from within.

This makes you the vibrational match for what you desire.
And ironically, it makes you no longer dependent on it from the outside.

I recommend visualizing before bed, and anytime during the day you feel disconnected from your vision.

Let your imagination lead you to peace, joy, confidence — now.
You don't wait for it to happen.
You become it.

> *"...This vision is for a future time. It describes the end, and it will be fulfilled. If it seems slow in coming, wait patiently, for it will surely take place. It will not be delayed."* — Habakkuk 2:2–3

DAILY TREASURE HUNT

This is one of my favorite practices.
It's called the **Daily Treasure Hunt**, a mental practice coined by Dr. Daniel Amen — a brilliant brain expert.

Your brain is always looking for evidence to prove itself right.

Whatever you focus on, you'll find more of.

Have you ever spilled your coffee in the morning and felt like your whole day went downhill after that?
That's not a coincidence.

It's your brain subconsciously scanning for more negatives — because that's what you've tuned it to.

The good news?
You can train your brain to do the opposite.

Before you go to bed, replay your day in your mind and ask:
What went well today?
What did I do right today?
What am I grateful for?

Go on a treasure hunt to find all of the positive moments in your day.

Then I take it one step further:
Replay the moments you wish you'd handled differently.
Not to shame yourself — but to rewrite it.

For example, if someone was rude to you, and you were rude back.
Visualize how your higher self would have responded.

Would they take it personally, or recognize someone else's projection?
Your highest self would not match the energy of the miserable.

Teach your brain how to show up better next time.

> *"Finally, brothers and sisters, whatever is true,*
> *whatever is noble, whatever is right...*
> *if anything is excellent or praiseworthy—*
> *think about such things."*
> — Philippians 4:8

TRANSMUTATION

Transmutation is the simple act of turning one thing into another. In this case, we're talking about transforming negative emotions into positive ones.

This isn't toxic positivity.
It's not about ignoring what's hard or pretending everything is okay when it's not.

It's about **alchemizing** your pain instead of storing it.

Think of it as a 3-part emotional shift:

Negative → Neutral → Positive.

You can't always jump straight from sadness to joy or from anger to love.
And that's okay.

Start by sitting with the negative emotion or feeling.
Name it. Feel it fully.
Let it move through your body instead of getting stuck.

Take a moment.
Imagine a time you felt regret. Or embarrassed. Or hurt.
Do you feel it in your body?

If you don't process that energy, it stays stored—and could come out in moments you don't want it to.

That's why transmutation is such an important practice.
It allows you to release what you were never meant to carry.

Once the emotion becomes neutral, you can gently shift into something higher.
What did I learn from this?
How can I use this experience to grow?

Let your pain become your power.
Let your emotions become your teachers.

That's what transmutation is all about.

SELF CARE RITUALS

Do everything with intention.

Your showers are more than just hygiene, you can turn them into daily sacred rituals.

As you wash and rinse, imagine the water washing away stress, regret, or insecurities.
Imagine it cleansing the old version of you.

Not everything you feel belongs to you.
Wash away what's not yours.
Step out the new version, feeling renewed and more aligned.

Speak life over your body:
I love my clear, smooth, glowing skin.
I love my thick, healthy hair.
I am comfortable in my own skin.

Massage in your lotion slowly.

Get to know your own body.

Pour love into yourself with every touch.

Be present and take your time.

Breathe in the scents of the products you use.

Don't rush.

For some people this is the only time of your day you get to yourself.

Honor it.

Let your routine become a ritual.

One you look forward to — morning and night.

Do this daily, and you'll start to love the skin you're in.

The results will compound faster than you imagine.

> *"Do you not know that your bodies are temples*
> *of the Holy Spirit... Therefore honor God with*
> *your bodies."* — 1 Corinthians 6:19–20

BREATHWORK

Breathwork is the simple, practice of intentionally controlling your breathing.

It is especially powerful, because you can do it anytime, anywhere — and no one has to know.

There are countless techniques, but my two favorites are:

Box Breathing:
Inhale for 4 seconds
Hold for 4 seconds
Exhale for 4 seconds
Hold for 4 seconds

Use this anytime you need to feel centered or calm.

4-7-8 Breathing:

Inhale for 4 seconds

Hold for 7 seconds

Exhale for 8 seconds

This one is especially helpful for anxiety.

Longer exhales activate **your parasympathetic nervous system —** the part of you responsible for rest and relaxation.

If your heart ever feels like it's racing, try the 4-7-8 method or simply count longer exhales.

Within minutes, you'll feel your body begin to slow down.

Find whatever breathing technique works best for you, and you will always have a way to calm yourself in any situation.

JOURNALING

Journal your journey.

Not just for now, but so you can look back later and see how much you've evolved and how far you've come.

By journalling, you will start to notice your patterns, cycles you're stuck in, and moments of growth you might've missed.

You'll have proof of your mindset shifts.
Evidence of your manifestations.
Receipts of the transformation you once only hoped for.

Writing things down is like a mental release.
It gets the thoughts out of your head and on to paper.
It brings clarity.

It helps you understand yourself — your fears, your triggers, your progress.

You can also use journal prompts to guide your writing and go deeper.

This is especially powerful if you're beginning **shadow work**: the process of facing the parts of yourself you usually hide or repress.

Shadow work exposes the wounds that hold you back.
Journaling is one of the safest ways to begin healing them.

Most of my journal entries turn into prayers.
I start by writing what I've been thinking and feeling...
and clarity follows.
By the end, I'm asking God to show me the next step.

CHAPTER 5

THE COMPOUND EFFECT

The **compound effect** is the principle that small, consistent action that is repeated over time, leads to big results.

Your daily habits shape your future.
Your repeated thoughts create your mindset.
Your smallest decisions influence your path.
For better or for worse.

Nothing you do is neutral.
Every small decision is pushing you forward or pulling you back.

The **problem** or the **power** is in your **routine**.

If you smoke one cigarette, you probably will not get cancer.
If you eat one donut, you will not gain weight.

One poor decision does not stop your progress.
But repeating these actions daily will surely have negative consequences on your health.

On the flip side — Reading 10 pages of a book per day might not feel like much... But you will finish the book in 2 weeks.
If you didn't start, the 2 weeks would've still passed by — but with zero progress.

Small progress over time yields great results.

Inner work is Exponential

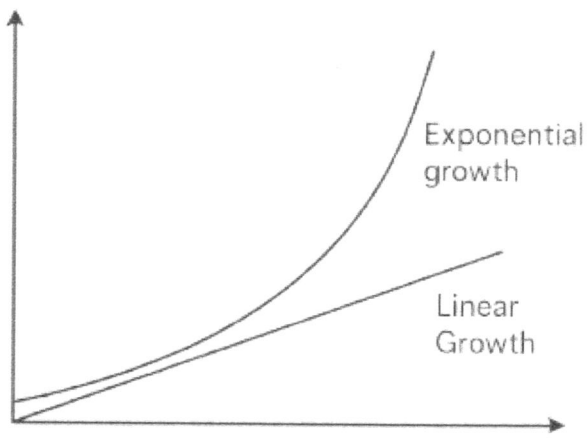

Exponential
growth

Linear
Growth

Our brains are wired to think linearly.
We can easily picture $8 + 8 + 8 + 8$.
But try $8 \times 8 \times 8 \times 8$ —much harder to grasp.

This is the nature of exponential growth:
It might not look impressive at first, until it multiplies.

Inner work is not linear, it's exponential.

You may even feel like things are getting worse before they get better.
But this is all part of the journey.

Your efforts are compounding— spiritually, mentally, emotionally.
Then one day, it will look like it all happened at once, but you will
know that it's what you've been working towards all along.

In the world of instant gratification we currently live in, try not to
romanticize the idea of overnight success.
Grow organically.

They say it takes 10,000 hours to master something.
With consistency, the student will eventually become the master.

> "You can be an extraordinary investor by earning **average** returns for an **above-average** period of time."
> — Morgan Housel, *The Psychology of Money*

In a simpler example, I went bowling with a group of friends.

Some of them would try to put a fancy spin on the ball or test new techniques. It looked impressive, and sometimes they'd hit a strike. But just as often, the ball would go right into the gutter.

I kept it simple. Straight down the middle — the exact same way, every time. I didn't get any strikes, but I knocked down 7 or 8 pins with every roll.

And guess who ended up winning the game? Me.

It didn't look impressive. But it was consistent — and **consistency wins**. Not just in bowling. In business. In growth. In becoming who you're meant to be.

A healed nervous system isn't a one-time quick fix.
It's the small, conscious choices you make every day that slowly compound into real, lasting peace.

Mindset shifts don't happen with the flip of a switch.
They happen by consistently catching your limiting beliefs, choosing a better thought, and doing it again and again, until your brain is rewired to believe in you.

Self-worth isn't rebuilt from one empowering quote.
It's the daily act of noticing the moments you shrink yourself, recognizing the lies you once believed, and starting to rewrite your inner dialogue.

Healing is the result of a thousand tiny moments where you choose a new way.

The compound effect gives us hope.

We don't have to be perfect — we just have to start.

Small steps, taken consistently, are powerful enough to change everything.

> *"Do not despise these small beginnings, for the*
> *Lord rejoices to see the work begin."*
> — Zechariah 4:10

CHAPTER 6

SOUL CLEANSE INVOCATION

An **invocation** is an intentional request— a call for help or guidance.

It's a moment to call on God's presence and align yourself with peace, purpose, and protection.

Think of it as a surrender that opens you up to receive.

Read this invocation out loud each morning and night for 30 days.

Be intentional.

Let it cleanse your energy, and prepare your soul to receive everything God has for you.

Dear God,

Please clear my soul of all trauma, past wounds, and resentments.
Please remove anything from my life that is no longer meant for me.
I now forgive all who have hurt me, and I retain the soul lessons I was
meant to carry forward.
I now forgive myself for all past mistakes, I release all shame and guilt.
I lovingly call back my energy from all people, places, habits, and situ-
ations that no longer serve me and my purpose.
Please release me from all ties and attachments that have kept my spirit
weighed down.
I lovingly sever any energetic cords that no longer belong to me.
May all negative emotions be transmuted into wisdom, and peace.
Cover me in Your divine force field of unconditional love and protection.
Help me to keep faith in you, God.
Help me to see the good in every situation.
Help me to find You in everything.
I submit to the present moment.
I let go of the need to control.
I know that all things are working in my highest favor.
I know that all paths lead to my desired reality.
I'm reclaiming my energy now.
I declare myself sovereign.
I declare myself whole.
I declare myself worthy.
Show me what my next step is, and I promise to obey.

Thank You.
And so it is.

CHAPTER 7

AFFIRMATIONS

Read these aloud every morning and night.
**Let them rewire your mind, align your frequency, and root you
in truth.**

I love myself.

I choose to embody the future version of myself now.

I am becoming the person I was created to be.

My past does not define me.

I release old beliefs that no longer serve me.

I am disciplined.

I am intentional with my time and energy.

I create habits that support my highest self.

I am consistent in the small things, because I know they compound.

I am grounded, focused, and committed to my growth.

I surrender control and embrace divine timing.

I am in alignment with my highest self.

I only attract people, experiences and opportunities that elevate me.

Anything I desire is available for me to have.

I trust God's timing for my life.

I am safe to expand, evolve, and elevate.

What is meant for me cannot miss me.

I deserve a life full of peace, love, and purpose.

Part II: The Journey

"To plant a garden is to believe in tomorrow."

— Audrey Hepburn

CHAPTER 8

THE PARADOX OF BEING

She is a paradox
A contradiction
She defies easy categorization
She is simple yet complex
She always understands, but rarely feels understood
Unpredictable, yet consistent
Alone, but surrounded by people
Confident, but overly self critical
Independent, but craves connection
Calm and composed, but fiercely passionate
Spontaneous, but carefully plans out her days
Logical and realistic, but delusionaly optimistic
Thinks a thousand thoughts, but says nothing

I wrote this before starting my inner work journey.

I never felt seen, I always felt "in between".

I longed to be understood— not just by others, but also by myself.

Now when I read it I can see that I understood myself all along.

I am a paradox — I do not wish to be easily defined.

I am authentic to the present moment — ever changing and evolving.

I recognize that **life is full of paradoxes**:

To receive, you must first let go.

Ball up your fist like you are holding on to something.

There is no room in your hand to receive more.

Now release it.

Let go, and open yourself up to receive.

The more you learn, the more you realize you don't know.

Before success, you will often fail.

The more you give, the more you receive.

The quieter you become, the more you hear.

Everything is temporary, yet everything you do matters.

Wanting a positive experience is a negative experience, but *accepting* a negative experience is a positive one.

On the surface, life seems to operate in contrast—opposites like light and dark, good and bad.

But when you look deeper, you realize these aren't opposites at all.

They are expressions that coexist, depend on each other, and reveal one another.

This is the concept of **non duality.**

To know good, you must know bad.
To know light, you must know darkness.
To know God, you must first lose yourself.

> *"For whoever wants to save their life will lose it,*
> *but whoever loses their life for me will find it."*
> — Matthew 16:25

When you let go of your **ego** and surrender your plans to God, you don't lose yourself — You uncover who you truly are.
You find the version of you that was made in His image.

Fear and faith are two sides of the same coin.
One cannot exist without the other.
Fear is simply faith misplaced.
Fear is belief in the worst. Faith is belief in the best.

> **"I know that I am happiness and I know that I am**
> **also suffering, that I am understanding and that**
> **I am also ignorance. For this reason I must take**
> **care of both of these aspects...I know that each of**
> **them is vitally necessary for the other."**
> —Thich Nhat Hanh, *True Love*

Happiness and suffering are two expressions of the same human experience.

Without sadness, joy wouldn't feel so good.

Without confusion, clarity wouldn't feel so grounding.

The truth is, some parts of the journey will feel contradictory.

The only thing constant in life is change.

They say, "The wise are the same in pleasure & in pain."
So we must learn to embrace life's uncertainty.

This is the heart of inner work.
Not to "fix" ourselves, but to hold space for every part.

Healing is not about becoming one thing, but embracing the fullness of who we already are.

Embracing your paradox is the first step to embracing your whole self.
The next is remembering who that self truly is.

CHAPTER 9

THE REAL YOU

I have mentors, read a lot of books, listen to podcasts, attend workshops, etc.

But one of my greatest teachers, and the source for my most profound realizations? My old journals.

I have evidence of my evolution on paper.
When I revisit my old entries I can see the shifts— my mindset and thought patterns, the way I live, love, and understand others, even my interests and hobbies.
All of it has transformed over the years.

I have always been this person deep down.

But for most of my life, she was hidden beneath programming, expectations, and limiting beliefs.

Sometimes, finding yourself isn't about becoming someone new.

It's about **unlearning** everything you were taught to believe about who you are that no longer aligns.

One of my favorite metaphors for this is from Michelangelo.

When asked how he created the *Statue of David* from such a massive block of marble, he said:

"I saw the angel in the marble and carved until I set him free."

Or, in another version:

"I removed everything that was *not* David."

So how did I become this version of me?

I removed everything that was not Madison.

Give yourself permission to let your old identity go.
It is safe to show up as *you*. The real you.

"Your handwriting. The way you walk. Which china pattern you choose. It's all giving you away. Everything you do shows your hand. Everything is a self portrait. Everything is a diary."
— Chuck Palahniuk

When you don't know yourself, you allow others to define who you are. You will absorb people's ignorant and conflicting ideas about you. You will start to take on the labels they place on you.
You unconsciously become a product of your programming.

But when you learn yourself, other people's opinions can no longer shape how you see yourself.

When you know yourself, on a deep and intimate level, that is when you are able to reclaim your power.

"If a man's concept of himself was different, everything in his world would be different"
—Neville Goddard, *The Power of Awareness*

So...who are you?

It seems like an easy question until you try to answer it.

We live in a world of information overload.

But the ones who *actually learn themselves* — who reflect on their **core beliefs and values** — are the ones who live in alignment with them.

We often incorrectly identify ourselves with our material possessions, our physical form, our achievements.

But this misidentification weakens our spiritual essence.

Turn your attention inward.
Ask yourself not what have you achieved or accumulated, but what is on the inside?
Not the fruit that your tree has produced, but the roots that hold you up.

***

Where your attention goes, energy flows.

When your attention is consumed by the external, it is like your energy is leaking.
You become disconnected from yourself and God.

You are innately worthy.
The God that created you is the same God who created the sun, moon and stars.
We are the walking embodiment of God consciousness.
It is up to us to realize who we are.

We don't rise to the level of our aspirations, we fall to the level of our self worth.

And remember: comparison is the thief of joy.
Don't ever compare yourself to someone else's curated self-expression, and especially not their portrayal of a perfect life on social media.

They say if everyone threw their troubles into a pile...
9 times out of 10, you would still choose your own.

"There's no such thing as a life that's better than yours. Love yours." — J. Cole

Journal Prompts:

Who am I when no one is watching?

What labels have I accepted that no longer feel true?

What are my values and core beliefs?

What version of me am I ready to release?

What version of me am I ready to step into?

CHAPTER 10

I AM

**"We are not nouns, we are verbs. I am not a thing -
an actor, a writer - I am a person who does things
- I write, I act - and I never know what I am going
to do next. I think you can be imprisoned if you
think of yourself as a noun."** —Stephen Fry

Confining yourself to a version of you that used to be true, but no longer is, is keeping your old frequency alive.

When you stop putting yourself in a box, you give yourself permission to be anything. You give yourself permission to evolve.

Be a person who does things, but don't attach your identity to it.

I am passionate about psychology, inner work and helping others.

A licensed esthetician who loves beauty and skincare.

I love fashion, music, art, and fitness.

I read, I draw, I write.

I am a daughter, a sister, a friend.

I am who I am.

Charles Horton Cooley said, "I am not what *I* think I am. I am not what *you* think I am. I am what I *think* you think I am."

Most of our identities have been rooted in perception rather than truth. We let what others think of us define ourselves.

People often say to just be yourself.

But this is bad advice for the person who does not know who they are.

You must first decide who you are, or rather who you want to be.

Declare your own "I am"s.

Neville Goddard taught that "I am" is the name of God within us.

What you attach to "I am" becomes your reality.

This is why affirmations are a sacred daily practice (see Chapter 4).

Never end an "I am" statement with something you would not want to come true.

Don't say, *"I am tired," "I am broke,"* or *"I am ugly."*
You are speaking those things over yourself.

When you're sick, don't say *"I am sick,"* say *"I am healing."*

Even "I will be" is a confession that *"I am not."*

If you *want* something, then you are separate from it, and you emit the frequency of lack.

And lack attracts more lack.

The Backwards Law by Alan Watts teaches:

The more you chase something, the more you push it away.

Wanting it too badly creates resistance.

But when you let go — what you desire can come naturally.

The end of wanting is being.

GOD'S "I AM"

"I Am Who I Am."
— Exodus 3:14

This is one of the most profound and mysterious declarations in Scripture.

When God says, *"I Am Who I Am"*,
He's revealing His essence: eternal, unchanging, and limitless.
He doesn't define Himself by comparison or category.
He simply *is*.

You don't get to decide who God is —
but **you do determine who He is *to you*.**

If you believe He is judgmental, you will judge yourself.

If you believe He is vengeful, you may live in fear or self-sabotage.

If you believe He has limitations, you will block your own blessings.

But if you believe He is loving, merciful, wise, abundant, and kind —
That's the experience you'll receive.

Whatever you need Him to be, He already is.

Do you need a Father? He is.

A teacher? He is.

A healer? He is.

Your perception determines your reception.

Chapter 11

✧ ✧ ✧

Perception & Perspective

Perception is how you interpret what you see.
Your eyes are not cameras, they are projectors.

The way you perceive the world is a projection of what's going on in your mind.

Your childhood, your beliefs, your trauma, your programming— they all taint your lens.

Psychology calls this *selective perception* —
your brain notices and interprets the world through the lens of your past experiences, emotions, and expectations.

Whether someone sees the glass as half empty or half full, both are technically correct. What matters is *how* they see it.

Perception reveals inner beliefs.

Whatever you believe, you are right.

If you believe you can— you're right.
If you believe you can't— you're right too.

What we see shapes how we feel —
And how we feel shapes what we see.
Change your lens, and you change your life.

Social psychology also explores the **expectancy effect**.

If you go into a situation expecting a certain outcome, you'll often experience exactly that.

Not because it was destined, but because that is what you were tuned in to see.

This is the heart of the Red Car Theory.

If you decide you want a red car, you then start to see them and notice them everywhere.

Are there actually more red cars now? No, your brain is just noticing them more now.

This is because of the Reticular Activating System (RAS), the part of your brain that filters the information you take in.

Whatever you focus on, your brain highlights.

So choose to focus on what you *want*, not what you fear.

When you understand this concept, you are freed from other people's negative opinions about you.

Because you know what they're seeing is just a projection.

It's a reflection of their own inner world.

You realize everyone is speaking from their past experiences, and current knowledge.

Which is why we must stop taking things personally.

Don Miguel Ruiz puts it perfectly in *The Four Agreements*:

> **"Nothing other people do is because of you. It is because of themselves. All people live in their own dream, in their own mind; they are in a completely different world than the one we live in. When we take something personally, we make the assumption that they know what is in our world, and we try to impose our world on their world."**

And so it is with the good you see in the world.

If you see beauty in something, you are projecting the beauty of your own heart.

Perspective is your viewpoint.

DawnCheré Wilkerson, author of *Slow Burn*, beautifully illustrates the power of perspective through a story in the Bible.

God instructed Moses to send 12 men to scout out the Promised Land, Canaan. This land was a gift from God. It was described as flowing with milk and honey — full of abundance.

When the spies returned, 10 of them only focused on the *giants* who lived there. They were scared and full of doubt.

Only two — Joshua and Caleb — believed they could take the land. They were looking through **God's perspective**, not human fear.

But the people listened to the fearful majority.

They let fear overrule their faith.

And as a result, they missed out on what God had for them.

They wandered for 40 years — and it wasn't until the next generation that the Promised Land was finally claimed.

They blocked their own blessings, not because God changed His mind, but because they couldn't shift their perspective.

With God inside of us we are invited to view the world through His eyes, not just our own.

It's not about how big the giants are.
It's about how vast the land is.

And so it is with our lives.

Don't focus on how big your problems are.
Focus on how beautiful your blessings are.

CHAPTER 12

✧ ✧ ✧

REWIRE YOUR BRAIN

On average, humans have 60,000-80,000 thoughts every single day.

How many of those thoughts are negative?

And how many of them do you repeat over and over?

It's time to flip the script...

Flip the Script

Your **conscious mind** is the part of your mind you're aware of.
It's where you think, reason, and make decisions.

Your **subconscious mind** is the deeper part of your mind that runs in the background.
It stores your beliefs, memories, emotional reactions, habits, fears, insecurities, and self-image.

Think of your subconscious mind as the way your brain has been **programmed**.

It is *always* active and controls about 95% of your thoughts, feelings and decisions.

How is it programmed?

Environment & upbringing from ages 0-7
Repetition (what you hear, see and say often)
Emotionally charged experiences

For the first 7 years of life your brain is most plastic — meaning flexible and absorbent.
During this time you're mostly in theta brainwaves, which means **everything you saw, heard, or felt was absorbed directly into your subconscious**, with little to no filter.

Whether you know it or not, your upbringing has significantly impacted the way you view yourself and the world.

Repetition also has a powerful influence.
Science shows that the more you hear something, the more you believe it to be true. Your routines — and the words consistently spoken by the people closest to you — shape your internal beliefs.

Emotionally charged experiences rewire even faster than repetition. Think about people who suffer from PTSD — One highly emotionally charged experience altered their life significantly.

Trauma imprints fast. It alters your subconscious, and in turn, your daily thoughts and reactions.

Your external reality reflects what's stored in your subconscious.

Most of this programming was not your fault.

But it is up to you to take responsibility for your healing.

People often say, *"This is just how I am."*
No — that's just how you've been wired.
And wiring can be changed.

Neuroplasticity is your brain's ability to change, adapt, and rewire itself.

Your brain is capable of incredible change.
Dr. Joe Dispenza says, "What fires together, wires together".
When two neurons activate together, they strengthen their bond.

Through conscious effort, you can form new neural pathways that support your highest self.
You can reinforce the pathways aligned with the future you want — and weaken the ones keeping you stuck.

If you think thoughts of abundance, confidence, or joy — *with emotion* — you build that wiring.
You are literally teaching your brain a new way of being.

How to rewire your thoughts:
Become aware of your patterns — recurring thoughts or emotions
Interrupt the pattern — acknowledge that it is not true
Replace it — with a new thought or emotional response
Stay consistent — each time you override your programming, you weaken the old loop and strengthen the new one

See Chapter 4 for tools to reprogram your subconscious.

If you don't become aware of your programming, you'll keep running it on repeat—without even knowing it.

Autopilot

Autopilot is when you live life unconsciously.

You do the same things, think the same thoughts, and feel the same feelings everyday without realizing it.

When you live like this, the same circuits in your brain are being fired over and over, strengthening those patterns.

Your brain is mostly a product of the past.

When you live life on autopilot, your past is creating your future.

Joe Dispenza's **Thought Loop** explains how this works:

You have a thought

↓

That thought creates a **feeling**

↓

That feeling influences your **behavior**

↓

The behavior produces an **experience**

↓

The experience **reinforces** the original thought

↓

And the loop begins again...

Over time this loop becomes your identity.
Most people live in this loop **unconsciously**— repeating the same
thoughts, feelings, and actions every day.
This creates the **same reality**, day after day.

> **"The fact is, there's no room for the unknown in
> a predictable life."**
> — Joe Dispenza, *Becoming Supernatural*

By interrupting autopilot, you open yourself up to *infinite possibilities*
of a better future.

By changing your **internal state**, you can change your external world.

ADDICTED TO SUFFERING

It's frustrating, but true — we can be addicted to suffering.

Obviously we do not want to suffer, yet we can be subconsciously addicted to it.

The truth is, our brains are not wired to thrive, they are wired to survive.
Survival seeks safety.
Repetition creates the illusion of safety.

So if you've lived in sadness, fear, or anger for years...
Any higher emotion will feel unsafe — even joy.

To break the addiction you must become the observer of your mind.

You are not your thoughts, you're the one noticing them.
Change the thought "I am a failure" to "I am having the thought that I am a failure".

You are not your emotions, you are the observer of your emotions. Think of an emotion as getting on a train labeled with the emotion you're feeling. You didn't *become* angry — you just boarded the 'anger train.' And you can step off whenever you choose.

Don't try to prove your negative thoughts right. Prove them wrong. Ask: *"Is the opposite also true?"*
If you think: *"I always mess up,"* ask, *"When have I gotten it right?"*

Eliminate black-and-white language: *never, always, everyone, no one.* Sometimes we exaggerate situations to validate our emotions. You don't have to ignore your emotions — just see them for what they are by becoming the observer.

The moment you choose to observe instead of react—you take your power back, and the rewiring begins.

New Mind, New Life

You are not stuck.
You are simply repeating patterns.
And patterns can be changed.

Every word you speak to yourself is either strengthening your old frequency or building the new one.

The old version of you will try to pull you back.
It's familiar. It feels safe.
It will whisper lies, distort truths, and tempt you to go back to what's comfortable.

But **comfort isn't where transformation happens.**

To build a new life, you must first build a new mind.

When you rewire your brain, you shift your frequency.
When you shift your frequency, you change what you attract.
And when you change what you attract, you change your life.

> *"Do not conform to the pattern of this world, but be transformed by the renewing of your mind."*
> — Romans 12:2

> *"Put off your old self...be made new in the attitude of your minds; and to put on the new self, created to be like God in true righteousness and holiness."* — Ephesians 4:22–24

A new mind unlocks a new life.

This does not mean it will always be easy, but it *is* possible.

And the work starts now.

Chapter 13

Divine Delays

There is nothing on earth that blooms all year long.

Everything has its season.

There is a time to plant, a time to wait, and a time to harvest.

The day you plant the seed is not the day you harvest the fruit.

Recognize what season you're in, and give yourself grace.

Social media constantly shows us everyone's harvest.

But we didn't see them plant the seed.

We didn't see them water it every day.

We didn't see their discouragement while waiting for it to bloom.

All we see is the fruit — the highlight reel.

Sometimes, we feel jealous of someone else's success. But the truth is we have no idea how long it took them to get there.

Cherry blossoms bloom beautifully for only 1–2 weeks a year.
During that time, people travel to see them, have festivals, and take photos.
But the rest of the year? They're mostly ignored.
It's the same tree — just not in bloom.

People tend to show up when you're thriving.
They celebrate your wins, not your waiting.
Don't let that fool you into thinking you need to always be in bloom.

The point is:

Don't compare your season of patience to someone else's season of harvest.

Sometimes the best thing you can do right now is plant a seed.

***

Sometimes God will stretch you, challenge you, or reroute you — not to punish you, but to get you where you're meant to go.

He will repurpose the skills you learned in one season for your assignment in the next.
There is no such thing as a wasted season.
He's preparing you now... because you'll need it later.

Every calling comes with some degree of hardship.

You may think you're ready for the calling — but are you ready for the struggles that may come with it?

You want the success — but are you built for the spotlight?

You want the role — but do you want the responsibility?

Take Joseph's life in the Bible:

He was betrayed by his brothers, sold into slavery, and wrongfully imprisoned.

But every "setback" was a step toward his ultimate position of power.

Setbacks are divine setups.

Had he not been enslaved, he would have never entered Pharaoh's household.

Had he not been imprisoned, he would have never interpreted dreams for the king's officials.

Had he not been forgotten, he wouldn't have been remembered at just the right moment.

What looked like delay... was divine alignment.

Rejection is divine redirection.

Sometimes what you think you want is not what God has for you. And what He has is always greater.

***

Don't confuse divine delays with procrastination or misalignment.

Procrastination is stagnant energy.
It often happens when the action you're trying to take doesn't match your current frequency.
If your frequency is unmotivated, but your calling requires discipline, it might feel misaligned.

True misalignment feels like a contradiction to your highest self — like a diversion away from the person you're becoming.

Sometimes, when you move forward in a powerful, aligned direction — you might feel a reactionary pushback.
That's not always a sign to stop. It's just resistance to your growth.

Keep your eyes on the push from God — not the minor push-back from the enemy.

One thing that confuses the enemy?
When you stay positive in the middle of disappointment.
He thought the delays would break you.
But you stayed faithful.

Your faith will always beat the enemy's strategy.
Because you know setbacks are actually set ups.

***

There may be seasons where everything seems to fall apart.
You lose friends, relationships, opportunities.
But is it really a loss if it was never meant for you to begin with?

And what if what God has for you is ten times greater?

> **"Anything that is no longer in a vibrational match between you and your future is going to fall away. Let it. Don't try to put your old life back together because you're going to be way too busy with the new destiny you're calling to yourself."** — Joe Dispenza, *Becoming Supernatural*

Every loss is a gain.
Every removal is a divine rearrangement.
Sometimes, what feels like loss is actually **deliverance from delusion.**

> *"I am the true vine, and my Father is the gardener. He cuts off every branch in me that bears no fruit, while every branch that does bear fruit he prunes so that it will be even more fruitful."*
> — John 15:1–2

God will remove what no longer serves us

He prunes us, not to punish — but to prepare.
To make room for the fruit we're called to bear.

What feels like a delay is often **divine preparation.**

God's timing for your life is never late.

PRAYER FOR CLARITY

Dear God,

Please bring clarity into this situation.
Clear the noise, calm my thoughts, and align me with Your voice.
Please bless me with renewed vision and a clear calling from You.
Please fill me with Divine wisdom, not of the world, but from You.
Help me to be still in Your presence, so I can hear You clearly.
I trust that everything is happening in the best way, at the best time.
Please show me a clear sign.
If it is from You, let it feel peaceful and aligned.
I trust Your guidance.
Help me to release control.
Help me surrender my timeline, my fears, and my expectations.
Guide my next step, Lord.
Clear the path for me.
Let every move I make reflect trust in You.

Amen

CHAPTER 14

AFFIRMATIONS

I am whole, worthy, and loved — exactly as I am.

I release every label that no longer aligns with who I'm becoming.

I am authentically me.

I live in accordance with my values.

My mind is aligned with growth, peace, and purpose.

I am safe to rewire my mind and build new patterns.

Delays are not denials — they are preparation.

I am happy in the waiting.

What is meant for me will never miss me.

I release control and embrace God's perfect plan.

PART III: THE BECOMING

"You've changed." — Caterpillar

"We're supposed to." — Butterfly

Chapter 15

Journey > Destination

"Please don't spend your life convincing your-self that love or joy is reserved for the idealized version of you that only exists in the future"
—Unknown

Stop waiting to be happy *after* you achieve something.
Because once you get there, another goal will take its place.
The destination always moves. It's elusive.

Chasing happiness through external things is a trap.
There's always a next level.
A newer job. A nicer apartment. A better relationship.
And every time you arrive, it still doesn't feel like enough.

**What you're really chasing isn't the destination —
it's the *feeling* you believe it will give you.**

You think you're chasing a certain amount of money in the bank, but what you're really chasing is *security*.
You think you're chasing a relationship, but what you really want is *to feel loved*.

But the truth is:
There's nothing out there to "get."
What you're looking for is already within you.
What you're looking for comes from God.

Reflect on what it is you're chasing in life, and figure out what *feeling* you believe it will give you.

Cultivate that feeling on the inside, and you'll stop being dependent on the outside.
You'll also become a match for more of what you desire.

**The more you embody the feeling now, the less you'll chase it —
and the more naturally it will come.**

Instead of obsessing over the destination, choose to be present for the journey.

The journey is your life.

***

The fact that you're reading this book tells me you have a growth mindset. You want to evolve, learn, and become more.

Choose to look at life as a series of peaks and valleys.
A never ending cycle of learning and mastery.

It's like a video game.
When you beat level one, you unlock level two.
And the next level is always slightly more challenging.

Some levels take longer to figure out; others are quick and easy.
But the goal is always the same: **progress**.

Imagine how boring it would be to keep replaying the same level over and over.
You must keep repeating the same level until you master it.

And so it is with life.

This is why people find themselves stuck in the same patterns or entering new relationships with the same type of person — the lesson hasn't been fully understood yet.
Until you learn, the cycle will continue.

God will not unlock the next level of your life until you've learned what this one is trying to teach you.

That's why self-awareness is so important: it's the key to breaking patterns and stepping into the next chapter God has for you.

That's why journaling is so important — it helps you spot patterns in your life.

It is easier said than done. This is just as much a reminder for myself as it is to the person reading.

But looking back, I can now see how every part of my journey was necessary.

Every book I read, every failed business venture, every person I met, shaped me into who I am today and prepared me for the next level.

Remember, all paths will eventually lead you to where you are supposed to be.

Every lesson prepares you for what's next.

And every level builds the wisdom needed to carry the weight of your calling.

We all have an inner critic holding us back thanks to something called the spotlight effect.

It tricks us into thinking everyone is watching us, when really, most people are focused on themselves.

Don't let the imaginary spotlight stop you from trying.

It's okay to mess up. It's okay to fail.

The only thing you'll regret is not trying.

Don't look back one day thinking, *If only I'd tried a little harder...If only I'd given 100% instead of holding back.*

You may never get over the fear.

Learn to go for it anyway.

Learn like you'll live forever.
Live like you'll die tomorrow.

You will get to where you're meant to go.
But don't miss your life, because you're too focused on a destination.

The "good old days" are happening right now.

Enjoy the ride.

And if someone asked me,
"What's more important: the journey or the destination?"
I'd say... it's the people you take with you.

Journal Prompts:

What patterns am I repeating?

What feeling am I searching for?

What lessons might God be asking me to learn right now?

What do I need to overcome to unlock the next level in my life?

CHAPTER 16

RAISE THE BAR

"Your "**container**" is your energetic and emotional set point of how good you will allow your life to get." —Mina Irfan, *Lady Balls*

Expanding your energetic container is the process of outgrowing the old you, and raising the standards for your life.

Sometimes, you unconsciously have a cap on what you think you are worthy of receiving.

Placing a cap on what you believe you're allowed to receive underestimates the generosity of an infinitely abundant God.

The best example to explain this concept is lottery winners who grew up in poverty. Studies indicate that nearly one-third of lottery winners go bankrupt within three to five years.

They do not have the energetic threshold that is big enough to hold such wealth.

They won all of the money they needed to live comfortably for the rest of their life. But because their frequency was still aligned with being broke, that is what they eventually brought back into their life experience — even after winning millions of dollars.

When you become complacent, your container is full and there is no room for growth.

You expand your container by getting out of your comfort zone.

This creates energetic space for bigger blessings.

Stretch your capacity for what you allow yourself to receive.

Do your expectations align with what you believe you are worthy of?

Do you desire help but turn it down when it is offered?

Do you say you want your partner to spoil you with gifts, but have a hard time even receiving a compliment?

One way to do this is to normalize your blessings.

Replace the language you use when something good happens.

Make the switch from "Wow this is crazy" to "This is amazing and it's right on time."

Another way is to ask the question: *Why not me?*

If it can happen for someone else, then why can't it happen for me?

Someone has to get the front parking space, so why not me?

Someone is going to get a promotion at work, so why not me?

People experience miracles everyday — why not me?

There is nothing noble about dimming your light, and pretending to be less than God made you to be.

In fact, it is disrespectful.
Walk in your purpose with your head held high.

I was not made to be mediocre.
Greatness is an expression of Godliness.
To embody greatness is to embody God.
Greatness from God's perspective is a return on *His* investment in me.

My potential is God's gift to me,
What I do with it is my gift to God.

When you raise the ceiling for what blessings you allow yourself to receive, you raise your standards, and you raise your frequency.

But remember: when you raise the ceiling you must not forget to also raise the floor.

The floor is the bare minimum of what you will accept for yourself.
When you don't raise the floor, you leave too much room for self sabotage.
Don't leave any room to go back to the old you.
Don't fall back into old habits.
It's easy to fall back into your comfort zone, but going back will only delay your blessings.

"No one pours new wine into old wineskins. Otherwise, the new wine will burst the skins; the wine will run out and the wineskins will be ruined."
— Luke 5:37

This verse is part of a parable Jesus used to explain that **new things need new containers**.

To understand his message, it will require a new mindset.
To receive abundance and blessings, you must become someone capable of holding them.

God wants to pour new blessings into your life — but first, you must become a new vessel.

Like new wine in old wineskins, your old beliefs can't carry where He's trying to take you.

It's time to raise the bar.

And expand your container.

CHAPTER 17

DIVINE ALIGNMENT

Vibrational alignment means your thoughts, emotions, and energy are in sync with what you want to attract in your life.

In a world where most people are performing for approval — Be the person who cares more about how their life *feels* than how it looks.

Do the things that align with your soul.

People have become very good at making their life look peaceful and perfect on social media, but you never know what they're experiencing internally.

It's easy to pretend that you have it all together.
It's easy to make it look like you're living your best life.

But **how your life feels to you matters more than how it looks to others.**

If there was no social media, if you couldn't post your every move —
Would you still be doing some of the things you've been doing?
Or is some of it just for show?
What truly bring you joy?

Anything done out of alignment with your higher self is pulling you further from your purpose.

Even if it feels good in the moment... don't satisfy every desire.
Temporary pleasure isn't worth permanent misalignment.

Authenticity keeps you in alignment with God's plan for your life.

No amount of external validation from a curated, inauthentic self presentation will ever compare to the peace of being yourself.
Authenticity is how you stay in step with divine timing.

The more true you are to yourself, the more magnetic you become to the right people and opportunities.
And the more naturally you repel what's not for you.

Another way to understand alignment is through **synchronicities** — or meaningful coincidences.

Carl Jung says, "Thus, we may say that the Divine does not speak in words. It speaks in synchronicities."

He believed the unconscious mind and the external world align in "mysterious ways".

Have you ever had a moment where it feels like everything's just falling into place? That's alignment.
Start noticing these synchronicities in your life.

No one else can tell you what is or isn't aligned with your soul. It's an unexplainable feeling in your body.

Notice that I am explaining it as a **feeling in your body** rather than thoughts in your head.
Your head is often clouded with outside opinions, programming from your childhood, limiting beliefs, half truths you've learned from social media, etc.
But your body knows.
Learn to trust what it is communicating to you. And don't ignore it.

Ever had a strong gut feeling not to go somewhere — then later realized why? That's not anxiety — that's your **intuition**.
Learn to trust it.
It can only guide you if you listen to it.

***

You won't have to force what flows.
You won't have to chase what is aligned.

Every decision you make should move you closer to purpose.

Be intentional with your energy.

119

Everything is energy.
And **energy without intention wanders.**

Emotions are energy in motion.

Your emotions are one of the clearest indicators for what is a vibrational match to your higher self.
When do you feel most alive?
When do you feel most drained?

When something feels good, trust it. If it's not a 100% yes, it's a no.

When something feels bad it shows a divergence from your higher self.

If you're aligned, your efforts will feel like devotion — not depletion. It will energize you and fill you with joy and pride.

I have seen this in my own life through many failed business endeavors that were not aligned with my soul.

When I write a paper for school on a topic I don't care about, it's exhausting. But when I write this book — the words flow.

Hard work only works if you're working hard at the right thing.

Alignment feels like floating downstream — letting go of the paddles, and moving with God's current.

Resistance feels like rowing upstream — tiring, draining, and going nowhere.

> **"When you achieve vibrational alignment, any inspired action will feel wonderful. Without the vibrational alignment, any action taken will feel difficult. With the vibrational alignment, your effort will yield wonderful results or return on your time. Without the vibrational alignment, the outcome of your effort will be disappointing, resulting in discouragement as you conclude, "This just doesn't work for me.""**
> — Esther and Jerry Hicks

They go on to explain that vibrational alignment feels like relief. Like peace. Like flow.

Nothing your highest self truly wants is upstream.

Let go. Let God guide the current.

***

Here's a way to check in with yourself:

Think of someone you admire.
If they saw your phone, your conversations, your weekends, your habits... What would they think about you?
Would it make them impressed or disappointed?

Who are you when no one's watching?

Anything you wouldn't want them to see is a space for growth.
Not because you need to impress anyone.
But because your soul is calling you into deeper **integrity**.

Be someone you're proud to be — even in private.

When your values and actions line up, that's integrity.

And when you live with integrity, you unlock the kind of confidence
that can't be faked — because it's grounded in divine alignment.

Living in integrity is embodying your values.
It's when you go from knowing better to being better.

Chapter 18

From Knowing to Being

No one talks enough about the space between *knowing* something and actually *living* it in real time.

Learning is only step one.
Anyone can read books, memorize information, or even articulately speak about something — but embodying it? That's the challenge.

It's frustrating to watch yourself repeat old patterns, even after all your growth.
You may start to notice what you *could have* said or done differently after the moment has passed.
You knew better, but you acted the same.

That awareness is progress.
Give yourself grace.
Reflect on it, rehearse how you would handle it differently, and then do better next time.

What's even more freeing is when you're mid-pattern and realize —
Wait... I don't actually feel this way anymore.

It was your old self showing up out of habit.
And in that moment, you have the power to pause, and respond as the person you're becoming.

To embody something is to become the living example of it.
It's expressing something through your actions and behavior.

It's one thing to say you have faith, and it's another to live like it.
It's one thing to say you're confident, and it's another to live in confidence.

Confidence is not walking into a room thinking you're better than everyone else. It's not having to compare yourself at all.

Confidence comes from knowing you were created in God's image. Knowing that you are God's masterpiece. That your worth is not up for debate.

Confidence should be innate, but the world tries to take it from us.
Comparison chips away at it daily.
But you can build it back — through faith and aligned action.

Confidence grows with practice.
Cook more, and you'll grow confident in the kitchen.
Speak more, and you'll grow confident in your voice.

Say you'll do something — and actually do it.
Every follow-through builds self-trust.

Try it:

Read a book cover to cover.

It releases dopamine, gives you a tangible win, and the book becomes a symbol of follow-through.

Make a to-do list and check things off.
Each checked box releases dopamine and reinforces confidence.

Set short-term goals that move you toward your long-term vision.
Each small win compounds.

Confidence is quiet. Insecurity is loud.

Notice that liars tend to over explain, and people that are telling the truth don't care whether they're believed or not.
The people with real wealth are often the ones dressed simply and put together. The flashiest ones are usually the ones faking it.
Gunna said it best: "Why the brokest the loudest in the room?"

True confidence is an inner knowing.

You have nothing to prove — you just are.

"It's easy to be a boss in a room full of lames.
But are you still a boss in a room full of bosses?"

It's easy to feel secure around people doing less than you.
But true confidence shows up around people doing more —
And feels *inspired* rather than inferior.

***

My favorite embodiment technique is **"The Marilyn Effect"**.
Marilyn Monroe had a way of turning on and off her aura.
She turned it off so that she could go in public and not be recognized.
She could turn it back on by shifting her posture, focus, and energy, and suddenly be seen.

It wasn't about her outer appearance, but about her **intentional embodiment**.

I've personally tried this, and it works! You can try it too.
Walk into the grocery store normally— in a rush, looking down at your phone. You'll likely go unnoticed.

Now try again: Slow down. Fix your posture, and hold your head up.
Focus on how you feel, not what others are thinking.
Smile. Walk with presence.
I guarantee people will notice you.

When you stop observing others — *you* become the one being observed.

Focus on you.

And watch the difference in how people treat you...

Energy doesn't lie. Aura can't be faked.

According to the HeartMath Institute, the heart generates an electro-magnetic field that radiates several feet from the body.
This field holds emotional information — and influences how others feel around you.

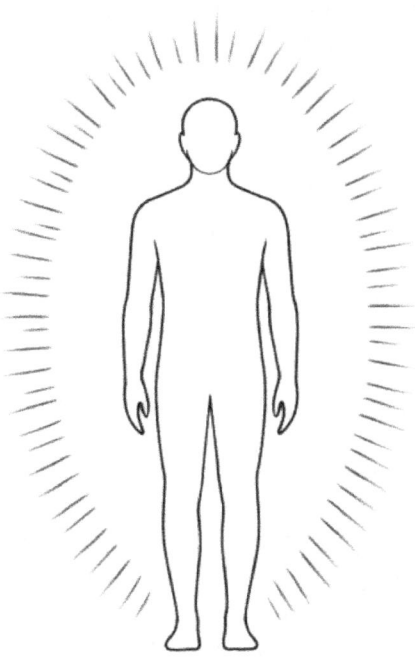

This electromagnetic field can be conceptualized as your **aura**.
It's made of your self image, your self concept, your frequency.

People feel your frequency before you say a word.

Your emotions are the largest shareholder of your frequency.

Remember that emotions are energy in motion.
Energy in motion becomes a vibration.
A vibration that continues long enough becomes a frequency.

Emotional intelligence is the ability to recognize, understand, and **manage** your emotions.

It's not just psychology, but it is spiritual hygiene.

It helps you to radiate the energy you want to attract.

***

Sometimes, there isn't more work to be done, just life to be lived.

Let yourself rest and demonstrate what you've learned.

Healing isn't always doing more, working harder, or fixing. Sometimes it's just being.

True healing is when you're at peace with where you currently are.

It is not about becoming more, it is about realizing who you already are.

If you are a better person today than you were last year, then you are moving in the right direction. Celebrate small shifts.

Acknowledge when you handle a situation better than you would have before. Those moments compound into a new identity.

Don't just learn it, live it.

Our goal isn't perfection — it's embodiment.

People can quote Scripture all day online — but are they *living* it? We know how Jesus lived — but are we living like Him?

We are called to embody Christ daily by:
Loving others deeply
Forgiving freely
Being honest and living with integrity
Treating everyone equally
Showing compassion
Obeying God

> *"Those who say they live in God should live their lives as Jesus did."*
> — 1 John 2:6

> *"Follow God's example, therefore, as dearly loved children and walk in the way of love, just as Christ loved us and gave himself up for us as a fragrant offering and sacrifice to God."*
> — Ephesians 5:1–2

CHAPTER 19

✧ ✧ ✧

LOVE

If you ask 50 people what their definition of love is, I bet you will receive 50 different answers.

Love shows up in so many different forms, but the English language reduces it to just one four-letter word.

The reality is, the root to **everything** is either love — or a lack of it.

Love shows up as kindness, patience, truth, peace, empathy...
Lack of love shows up as hate, fear, insecurity, jealousy, ego...

Every action is either an expression of love or cry for it.

A person who lashes out in anger is probably hurting deep inside.
Someone who is controlling might feel powerless inside.
Even manipulation or selfishness is often a distorted attempt to feel secure or seen— all cries for love in disguise.

So don't take people's poor behavior personally, and don't judge them. They're simply acting from a place where love is missing.

Remember the concept of non duality:
There is no true separation.

Behind hate is wounded love.
Behind jealousy is admiration.

People aren't inherently bad.
They are just deprived of love — and acting like it.

But when you are full of love, it overflows.

And you start to see it everywhere.

"Love is the bridge between you and everything."
— Rumi

To love is to know God.

"Dear friends, let us love one another, for love comes from God. Everyone who loves has been born of God and knows God. Whoever does not love does not know God, because God is love."
— 1 John 4:7–8

To know God is to recognize love in everything.

I see love in the way I take care of myself.
When I feel empathy.
When I am laughing with my friends.
When my cats cuddle with me.
When I see a couple holding hands.
In strangers showing kindness.
When someone remembers small details about me.

I believe in love, because of the way I love.
Love is everywhere, every single day.

All you have to do is look out for it.

***

I read something in *Think and Grow Rich* that completely changed my perspective:

"If you believe yourself unfortunate, because you have loved and lost, perish the thought. Love comes and goes as it pleases without warning. Accept it and enjoy it as it remains, but don't worry about its departure, this won't bring it back. All love experiences are beautiful and beneficial. No experience that touches the spiritual forces of the heart could ever be harmful. Love is life's greatest experience."

If love is spiritual, can it survive human mistakes?
Maybe we've misunderstood it entirely.
What if we're here to experience *imperfect* love —
What if real love is forgiving someone for being human?

> *"Make allowance for each other's faults, and*
> *forgive anyone who offends you. Remember, the*
> *Lord forgave you, so you must forgive*
> *others. Above all, clothe yourselves with love,*
> *which binds us all together in perfect harmony."*
> — Colossians 3:13–14

You cannot expect someone to love you when they haven't yet learned
how to love themselves.
So what if sometimes loving *yourself* means walking away?
Maybe the purest form of love is found in your ability to let someone
go when it's time.

People say they want unconditional love —
But maybe only **God** can give that kind.

The kind of love that asks for nothing in return.
The kind of love that is unchanging and keeps no record of wrongs.
That's the kind of love that lives inside you.

When you are in a state of love — toward God, others, or yourself —
You embody the highest frequency there is.
You experience *heaven on earth*.

Chapter 20

Found the God in Me

I don't know about you, but growing up I never felt close to God in the way others seemed to. My view of God was a big man up in the sky. When people would say they "heard God speak to them", I thought I was supposed to actually hear a man's voice.
God felt external. Distant. And separate from me.

It wasn't until years later that I realized God is inside of me.
That He wasn't far away, He was with me all along...
He is in the ocean and the sunset. In music and art.
In my intuition. In my heart.

God isn't somewhere out there.
God is everywhere.
God... is.

A DEEPER LOOK

I've found that sometimes it resonates most when I understand the stories in the Bible as **metaphors**.

They serve as spiritual manuals for navigating different seasons of life. Symbolic truths that mirror the inner journey of our own lives.

Healing the blind → God can restore our vision: the way we see ourselves, others, and our purpose in life.

Raising the dead → He can resurrect what we feel like we lost: our hope, our identity, our soul.

Parting the sea → He can make a way when we feel trapped or like there's no way out.

What I'm about to share next is known as an esoteric interpretation of Scripture with some metaphysical undertones.

Esoteric refers to **deep, symbolic,** or **inner knowledge** that isn't obvious to the general public. **Metaphysics** deals with the nature of **reality, consciousness,** and **existence**.

It is important to note here: **Interpretation should never be treated with the same authority of the written word.**

> *"Your kingdom come, your will be done, on earth as it is in heaven."* — Matthew 6:10

From this perspective, heaven can be understood as a state of mind. And as we've explored, the state of your mind influences how you experience life on Earth.

Therefore "on earth as it is in heaven" means o*n earth as it is in your mind* or: **as within as without.**

Heaven, in this sense, can be conceptualized as an inner state of peace, bliss, and harmony. It's love and compassion. Wisdom and alignment. It's non-attachment. It requires nothing external. It's fulfillment from within. It's *connection* to God.

Hell, by contrast, is inner turmoil. It's guilt, shame, lust, anxiety, scarcity...It's *misalignment* with God.
It's attachment to the material world and to your **ego**.

Most people want heaven, but their frequency is aligned with hell.

*"But seek first his kingdom and his righteous-
ness, and all these things will be given to you as
well."* — Matthew 6:33

We must first seek God —
And get into the consciousness (or frequency) of his kingdom.
Become fulfilled internally.
Only then will we have the ability to manifest our desires.

*"A man can receive nothing, except it be given
him from heaven."* — John 3:27

This verse reminds us that no matter how hard you hustle, your reality
won't truly shift until your inner world does.

This doesn't mean it won't still require aligned action —
But you can't outrun your frequency.

You must align with what you desire internally before it can manifest
externally.

Manifestations can only come when you align with God.

"For God so loved the world that He gave His one and only Son, that whoever believes in Him shall not perish but have eternal life." — John 3:16

This is the **Gospel.** The good news!
It is an invitation for eternal life —
An awakened state of inner peace, not just someday in heaven, but here and now.

This doesn't mean heaven and hell don't also exist in some future or eternal form —
But I'm inviting you to explore them as *internal realities* now.

"You won't be able to say, 'Here it is!' or 'It's over there!' For the Kingdom of God is already among you." — Luke 17:21

It's not just about going to heaven after death.

It's the recognition that **the Kingdom of God is within us, and we get to experience it now.**

Take a moment to think about something or someone that you love deeply or will trigger an emotional response.

Hold it in your mind in a way that makes you feel something.
And really feel it.

Do you hear that roaring in your ears?
Do you feel that sensation in your body?
That's not just a thought— that's energy in motion.

That is the power that our emotions have over our entire state of being.

Align your emotions with the frequency of your choice: an internal state of heaven or hell.

With God, we get to live in heaven on earth.

Inner Knowing

To dive a bit deeper:

Louis Sefer wrote in *Sacred Secrets of Esoteric Christianity,* that throughout time, some churches have replaced **gnosis** with **dogmas** that no longer reflect the true essence of Jesus's teachings.

Gnosis: Comes from the Greek word "knowledge", refers to spiritual insight— an internal knowing on a soul level.

Dogmas: Belief system respected as absolute truth by its followers

Some churches became more focused on dogmas —rituals, rules, and hierarchy. Than gnosis— a personal relationship with God and recognition of the divine within us.

To be clear, this is not to say I agree with the belief system that is Gnosticism, but the word gnosis itself offers a valuable perspective:

True spiritual wisdom is not what is taught and memorized, it's the awakening and embodiment of the inner knowing that is already inside of you.

This idea expands on my point that there is nothing to attain or "get" that is outside of us.

What we're searching for is already on the inside.

We just have to remember, or go deeper to find it.

What the world gives you, the world can take from you.

But what you know from within is yours forever.

You don't need permission to connect with God.

You don't need a title to carry wisdom.

THIRD WAY

There are two common paths people tend to follow in life, and you may find that you don't fully resonate with either one.
But the good news is that there's another way.
It's the way of Jesus. A life aligned with God.

Pastor Dharius Daniels calls this the **Third Way** —
a higher path that invites us beyond division, beyond ego.

There's **Culture's Way:** The way of the world.
It's the path that aligns with social norms and what the majority is doing. It emphasizes material success and external validation.

There's **Church's Way:** The way of religion.
It focuses on religious traditions and institutional practices. While this way is meaningful, it can sometimes become rigid or disconnected from personal transformation.

And then there's the **Third Way**.

This way is about living like Jesus.

Not just knowing Scripture, but embodying it.

It's inner transformation. Spiritual maturity. It's love, humility, truth, grace, and conviction lived out in everyday life.

Earlier I explored some different perspectives, not to diverge from the Christian faith, but to spark thought and look deeper.

Healthy faith walks between the extremes.

It lies within the tension of legalism and mysticism.

The Third Way invites you to walk *with* God, not just follow rules about Him.

You're allowed to ask, *"What does this story awaken in me?"* without losing sight of scripture's original meaning.

It's about **relationship over religion.**

It embraces spiritual insight while staying rooted in God's revealed truths.

YOUR DIVINE ESSENCE

"Then the Lord God formed the man from the
dust of the ground. He breathed the breath of life
into the man's nostrils, and the man became a
living person." —Genesis 2:7

We are made by dust, yet God breathed life into us.

We have a spiritual essence.

But we are also human.

We are born with primal instincts.

These instincts are not bad — they help keep us alive.

It's why a baby is born with the instinct to cry when it needs something, because it cannot speak yet.

We are wired for survival.

But we are not animals.

We are conscious beings.

If we lived only in survival mode, we would constantly react to perceived dangers and live in fear.

We would not get the full life experience we get to have when we acknowledge the divine part of ourselves.

The part that's loving, has purpose, and made for human connection.

As conscious beings we possess **imagination**.

God gave us this gift for a reason.

Not just to escape reality, but to reshape it.

He gave us the ability to see beyond our current circumstances and envision a better future — Not through ego, but through renewal.

"Though outwardly we are wasting away, yet inwardly we are being renewed day by day." —
2 Corinthians 4:16

Imagination is the starting point of this inner renewal.

It is how we begin to align with what *could be*.

When you imagine the best version of yourself —

You're not being unrealistic.

You're tapping into what's possible through God.

Imagination is not delusional or childish. It's Christ-like.

You weren't given this gift to imagine the worst case scenario.

You were given it to co-create with God.

So be sure to use it wisely.

TOGETHER AS ONE

"Enlightenment is when a wave realizes it is the ocean."
— Tich Naht Hanh

The truth is, once you accept that you are one with God, you are no longer separate from anything.

You are one with everyone and everything.

We are all connected, we all come from the same Source.

Therefore, when someone is experiencing hardship or failure — have **empathy**. For it could just as well be you.

When someone is successful, do not be envious, but rejoice with them! Let it be proof that it is possible for you too.

When you live from this awareness, comparison dissolves.
Gratitude grows.
Love expands.

That is what it means to be one with God:
To see the divine not just in yourself —
But in *everyone*.

To be one with everything means you are no longer separate from whatever it is you desire.
By becoming one with all, you get access to all.

Remain one with God, and through Him you can do anything.

> *"Remain in me, as I also remain in you. No branch can bear fruit by itself; it must remain in the vine. Neither can you bear fruit unless you remain in me. I am the vine; you are the branches. If you remain in me and I in you, you will bear much fruit; apart from me you can do nothing."* — John 15:4-5

THE GOD IN YOU

We often rush through life—scrolling, working, numbing, chasing.
If we aren't careful, we'll be too distracted to notice God's presence.

Every ordinary moment has the potential to become sacred if you slow
down...Look for the beauty in it.
Or rather... the **God** in it.

Most people won't notice, but *you* — you're not most people.
The fact that you've read this far says a lot.
The fact that you've taken the time to look within already sets you
apart. Most people aren't doing this kind of inner work.
This level of consciousness is rare.
So quiet your mind, because God is always speaking to you —
Through intuition, synchronicities, inspired thoughts, and the people
placed on your path.

It won't be a loud voice from the clouds,
But a gentle whisper from within.

"Do you not know that you are God's temple and that God's Spirit dwells in you?"
— 1 Corinthians 3:16

"And if the Spirit of him who raised Jesus from the dead is living in you, he who raised Christ... will also give life to your mortal bodies because of his Spirit who lives in you."
— Romans 8:11

"Do you not realize this about yourselves, that Jesus Christ is in you?"
— 2 Corinthians 13:5

"And this is the secret: Christ lives in you. This gives you assurance of sharing his glory."
— Colossians 1:27

So to the one finally stepping into their power...
Own it.

To the one who has reclaimed their light...
Let it shine.

To the one who has found God within...
Never forget it.

The kingdom was never far.
It's always been within.

And now...
You know how to find it.

Soundtrack

Get Well Soon — Ariana Grande

Stand Still —Maverick City Music

Go Baby — Cleo Sol

Just Like You — Keyshia Cole

Things Will Get Better — Cleo Sol

Stand — Donnie McClurkin

Bigger — Beyonce

No Child Left Behind — Kanye West

God Is — Kanye West

Life Will Be — Cleo Sol

Everything We Need — Kanye West ft. Ty Dolla $ign

All — Chandler Moore ft. Naomi Raine

Reason — Cleo Sol

Tell Him — Lauryn Hill

Calm & Patient — Jhene Aiko

Heaven is a Home... — Kali Uchis

Love Yourz — J. Cole

More Than Able — Elevation Worship

Ultralight Beam — Kanye West

Owe You Praise — Elevation Worship

ACKNOWLEDGEMENTS

To my parents—
Thank you for ensuring my first 7 years of life were full of peace and love, setting my nervous system up for a beautiful future. You always allowed me to be myself and pursue my dreams. Thank you for everything. I would not be where I am today without you both. I am eternally grateful for you.

To my mentor, Mina Irfan—
Thank you for teaching me the power of inner work, feminine energy, and spiritual alignment. You helped me identify and release the limiting beliefs that were holding me back, and guided me into becoming the woman I am today. Thank you for being my role model of what life can be when you live in alignment with God.

To my pastor, Dr. Darius Daniels—
Your sermons resonate with every fiber of my being. They have not only influenced my writing, but brought a new perspective into the way I view church, and the way I live my life. Thank you for helping me strengthen my relationship with God through your wisdom and delivery.

REFERENCES

Amen, Daniel G. *Change Your Brain, Change Your Life.* New York: Harmony Books, 2015.

Ash, Tim. *Unleash Your Primal Brain: Demystifying How We Think and Why We Act.* Costa Rica: Primal Brain Press, 2021.

Daniels, Dharius. *Sermons and Teachings.* Accessed 2024.

Dispenza, Joe. *Becoming Supernatural: How Common People Are Doing the Uncommon.* Carlsbad, CA: Hay House, 2017.

Goddard, N. (1952). *The Power of Awareness.* DeVorss & Company.

HeartMath Institute. *The Science of the Heart: Exploring the Role of the Heart in Human Performance.* Boulder Creek, CA: HeartMath Institute, 2022.

Hicks, Esther, and Jerry Hicks. *The Astonishing Power of Emotions: Let Your Feelings Be Your Guide.* Hay House, 2007.

Hill, Napoleon. *Think and Grow Rich.* Meriden, CT: The Ralston Society, 1937.

Housel, Morgan. *The Psychology of Money: Timeless Lessons on Wealth, Greed, and Happiness.* Harriman House, 2020.

Image created with assistance from ChatGPT (OpenAI), 2025.

Irfan, M. (n.d.). *Lady Balls: The feminine art of inner power.* The Universe Guru. ,

Nero Knowledge. *Outsmarting Reality* (Book & YouTube Channel).

Nhat Hanh, T. (2006). *True love: A practice for awakening the heart.* Shambhala Publications.

Ruiz, Don Miguel. *The Four Agreements: A Practical Guide to Personal Freedom.* San Rafael, CA: Amber-Allen Publishing, 1997.

Sefer, Louis. *Sacred Secrets of Esoteric Christianity.*

Shetty, Jay. *YouTube Channel.* Accessed 2024.

The Holy Bible. New Living Translation (NLT), New International Version (NIV), English Standard Version (ESV).

Tolle, Eckhart. *The Power of Now: A Guide to Spiritual Enlightenment.* Novato, CA: New World Library, 1999.

Wilkerson, DawnCheré. *Slow Burn: The Hidden Strength of Waiting on God.* Thomas Nelson, 2024.